Just the Same
on the Inside

Understanding diversity and supporting inclusion in Circle Time

Stories by ... George Robinson and Barbara Maines
Activities by Margaret Collins

Illustrations by Simon Smith

Paul Chapman
Publishing

D1333657

ISBN: 1 904 315 56 9

Published by Lucky Duck
Paul Chapman Publishing
A SAGE Publications Company
1 Oliver's Yard
55 City Road
London EC1Y 1SP

SAGE Publications, Inc.
2455 Teller Road
Thousand Oaks, California 91320

SAGE Publications India Pvt Ltd
B-42, Panchsheel Enclave
Post Box 4109
New Delhi 110 017

www.luckyduck.co.uk

Commissioning Editor: Barbara Maines
Editorial Team: Mel Maines, Sarah Lynch, Wendy Ogden
Illustrator: Simon Smith
Designer: Helen Weller

Printed in the UK by Antony Rowe Limited

© Dr Juan Bornman and Margaret Collins 2004

Contents

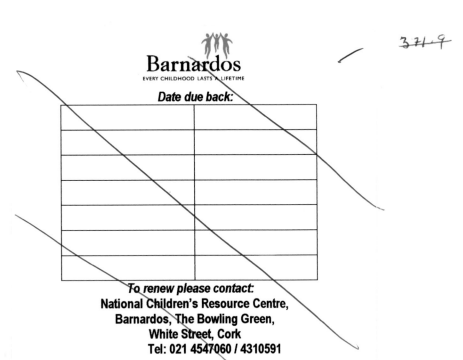

371.9

Introduction

Circle Time is increasingly seen as a time to talk with children about themselves, their classroom and other issues of the day. Within the structure of Circle Time most children feel secure to talk about relationships, rules, fairness and difficulties. It is also a time for children to reflect on their behaviour towards one another and towards those less fortunate than themselves. Their circle enables them to listen, to have their say and to consider how their actions impinge on others; how what they do and say affects the tranquillity or otherwise of the classroom.

Circle Time is therefore an ideal opportunity to present stories about children who have difficulties, problems, disabilities or who, for some reason, find it awkward or uncomfortable to settle easily into a classroom situation. By talking about these situations, using stories as a vehicle for discussion and following these with activities children can be helped to learn to understand and appreciate peers who are in some way different from themselves. Empathising with others and understanding their needs is good citizenship.

This aspect of citizenship is about being aware of, how to relate to, and how to treat other people, whatever their ability, colour, race or creed. Some children may not be taught this at home so it is essential to include it in everyday teaching at school. Much awareness of how to treat people is caught, not taught; it is therefore essential that teachers and all other people in school show their respect to those who have difficulties because of a disability, whether physical, emotional, a learning difficulty or a difference due to circumstances.

It is not easy to help children to feel good about themselves; it is even more difficult to help children with special needs to feel 'good enough'. Children with conditions that leave them challenged or who lack the ability to perform as well as other children need support not only from their teachers but also from their peers.

To achieve an inclusive society we need to help people to put themselves in the place of others, especially those with special needs, to learn empathic and caring responses. This has to begin in childhood and what better place than in the classroom?

This book has been written to help teachers, other adults working with groups of children and children in primary schools to understand some of the difficulties and conditions of those with special needs of various kinds.

This book is arranged in ten sections – about ten young people with very different and very special needs.

Each section has:

- ▸ an adult information page
- ▸ a story to be read to the children
- ▸ a set of activities for children aged 6 to 8
- ▸ a set of activities for children aged 9 to 11.

There is also a short list of books for suggested reading at the end of this introductory section.

The adult's pages contain supplementary information about the condition of the person in the story together with a few suggested websites and in some cases books that can help. There are many websites that older children can be encouraged to visit, not only the ones suggested, but others that they will find by using a search engine.

The children in these stories have special needs – the stories themselves will lead primary aged children to ask questions in order to gain an understanding of the conditions and the various needs of the children in the stories.

The activities have been planned to extend the main points of the stories and to give children something to do or practise that will help them to understand and empathise with the various conditions. Though they are arranged in two sets – one for younger children aged 6 to 8 years and one for older children of 9 to11 years, you may, depending on the abilities of the children in your class, want to dip into either section.

The activities would also be suitable for individual or small group work with children with special needs in your class, in special schools and in hospital schools. Your classroom assistant or special needs helper could help here with individual attention.

In some cases, the activities have direct links to activities in other sections and these are indicated on the adult's pages.

Some of the activities can lead to displays of children's work as a means of sharing the work with visitors, other adults and children in the school. Other activities can lead to projects that children can undertake as homework, holiday work or research at home with members of their family.

Older children who are more aware of news items on the TV, radio or in newspapers can be encouraged to learn about, and share, what is actually going on in the world with regard to people who are disadvantaged, disabled or displaced.

Acknowledgements for the Stories

Football Fun

Jill Rose, a physiotherapist with a lot of experience in this field, and friend who shares my passion for explaining disability to kids, worked with me on this story, giving me sound advice. Her insight, commitment and dedication to children with disability have always inspired me.

Magic Moments at Burger Bite

The input of Magda Lourens (formerly President of Down's syndrome South Africa, and the mum of an 11 year old son with Down's syndrome) is gratefully acknowledged. She helped me to understand this syndrome from a personal perspective and taught me what medical textbooks had failed to do, making this story one that many people can relate to.

Kyle and the Hairdresser

The input of Maureen Casey (remedial teacher) is gratefully acknowledged. Through her wealth of experience in this field, she made Kyle and the hairdresser come to life in my mind. Thank you!

Toni and the Boy who was Different

The input of Christine Koudstaal (Head: Unica School for children with Autism in Pretoria, South Africa) is gratefully acknowledged. She shared a wealth of knowledge and experience, shaping my thinking about autism.

My Sister Chantelle

The input of Joanne Atterbury (specialist teacher at the Memorial Institute for Child Health and Development) is much appreciated. She shared her experience in this field and provided many real life examples.

Books for suggested reading

Alcott, M. (1997) *An introduction to children with special educational needs*, Hodder & Stoughton, Abingdon.

Dare, A., O'Donovan, M. (1997) *Good Practice in Caring for Young Children with Special Needs*, Stanley Thornes, Cheltenham.

Feldman, W. (2000) *The Daily Telegraph*, Learning and Attention Disorders, Robinson, London.

Sainsbury, C., (2000) *Martian in the Playground*, Lucky Duck Publishing Ltd., Bristol.

Stakes, R., Hornby, G. (1996) *Meeting Special Needs in Mainstream Schools, A practical guide for teachers*, David Fulton, London.

Thacker, J., Strudwich,D. Babbedge, E., (2002) *Educating Children with Emotional and Behavioural Difficulties, Inclusive practice in mainsteam schools*, Routledge Falmer, London.

Football Fun

1. Football Fun

Information

The following story is about a boy who has cerebral palsy (CP). It is thought that about one in 400 people has this condition and nowadays fit well into mainstream schooling. It is important to help children to be aware of the difficulties of CP sufferers, to feel empathy for them and to understand ways they can help. The suggested activities reflect this need for awareness and understanding.

Some people with CP are of higher than average intelligence; other people with CP have moderate or severe learning difficulties. Most, like the majority of people without CP, are of average intelligence.

Cerebral palsy is a physical impairment that affects movement. It is not a disease or illness. Some movement problems are hardly noticeable but some are severe. All CP people are different, no two people with CP have the same difficulties,.

Cerebral palsy includes various conditions. There are three main types which correspond to damage in different parts of the brain:

 ▸ Ataxic CP presents as a balance problem. Sometimes there
   are shaky hand movements and difficulty with speech.

 ▸ People with athetoid CP lose some control of their posture
   and they often make unwanted movements.

 ▸ People with spastic CP have some muscles that are stiff and weak,
   especially when they move. This affects their control of movement.

CP has various causes:

 ▸ failure of a part of the brain to develop, either before birth or in early childhood

 ▸ complications in labour, premature birth or illness just after birth

 ▸ infections during pregnancy, infancy or early childhood,
   for example, meningitis or encephalitis

 ▸ occasionally CP is an inherited disorder.

Problems include difficulty with:

 ▸ walking, feeding, talking or using their hands

 ▸ sitting up without support – some need constant enabling

 ▸ sight, hearing, perception and learning

 ▸ epilepsy

- ▶ control of some movements and facial expressions.

There is a free CP helpline 0808 800 3333

Useful websites include:
www.scope.org.uk
www.ability.org.uk

LINKS with

- ▶ 'Akuti's New Talking Machine' activities
- ▶ modern inventions to help people with disabilities.

1. Football Fun

Daniel can never wait for Saturdays. He loves Saturdays. Not only because it is the first day of the weekend, but because it is the day on which he plays football. He is part of the Wimbledon football club and every Saturday morning at ten o'clock he proudly takes his place in the team. Their jerseys are red; he is glad about that because red is also the colour of his favourite team, Manchester United. Daniel dreams that one day when he's grown up he might even play for them.

This Saturday is special, because Daniel's team is playing a match against the Hampton club. He is not too worried about the match, because they have always been able to beat Hampton. As Daniel and his friends are busy warming up (basically all they do is jump up and down) Daniel notices the boy in the wheelchair next to the field. This boy fascinates Daniel because he is probably their most loyal supporter. He faithfully takes his place on the sideline every Saturday, never missing a match. Daniel has also noticed him at school. Although they are not in the same class, he knows that they are in the same year at school.

The whistle blows and the game starts. The red jerseys are all over the field, running and kicking the ball, while the blue jerseys are defending for dear life. Suddenly the Hampton striker gets the ball makes a run up the field and, can you believe it, scores the first goal! Daniel is worried. This shouldn't have happened. The game starts again; one of the Wimbledon wings gets the ball and starts dribbling it towards the goalposts.

"This is more like it!" Daniel thinks, whilst running behind his team-mate. But then, disaster strikes. The Wimbledon wing and Hampton defender collide. They both fall and the winger rolls about in pain. The trainer rushes on and helps him hobble off the field with what seems to be a sprained ankle. Daniel realises they will have to play with only 10 players. Suddenly an idea comes to mind. He walks over to the coach.

"Coach, I've been thinking. That boy over there in the wheelchair, he's in our school and I know that he's our age; can't we get him to play? He's here every Saturday, so I'm sure he knows the rules of the game!"

"A boy in a wheelchair, Daniel?" the coach was frowning. "How can we make that work? Surely if he's in a wheelchair he can't play football?"

"Well, coach, I don't know how. I just though it might be better having him in the team than having to play with only 10 players. I think it might be his dad with him, let's ask."

Reluctantly the coach walks with Daniel to the boy in the wheelchair. He talks to the boy's dad, "Sir, we've had a bit of an accident, as you saw. Daniel here wants to know if your son would like to play in Jason's place. He sprained his ankle really badly and won't be able to play for the rest of the day."

As the coach was talking, Daniel was watching the boy and noticed the broad grin breaking across his face. His arms were flapping wildly in the air.

"Coach, I am sure nothing would give Mark more pleasure, would it son? He has been coming here every week hoping for the opportunity to get on that field and play."

The coach was glad that he had listened to Daniel. "Well, I guess then the only thing left is for us to figure out how to make it happen," he said.

"We've thought about that," Mark's dad replied. Quick as lightening he took out some broad straps and firmly strapped Mark's body in the wheelchair. "There we go. Mark won't fall out and I'll push his wheelchair."

Just as abruptly as the game stopped, it started again. The red jerseys are all over the field once again. Mark's dad pushes him all over the field. The blue jerseys keep trying to cover all the gaps, but the red centre patiently waits, ready to strike. Somebody passes the ball to Mark.

"What will he do? How will he handle it?" Daniel wonders.

Daniel, together with the rest of the team, watch in awe as Mark's dad tilts the wheelchair back, allowing Mark to clasp his hands together and kick the ball with straight legs. The ball is now within kicking distance for the centre. The time has come; the goalkeeper loses concentration for a moment and the centre scores. One goal each and the whistle blows for the end of the game.

The Wimbledon team are smiling. An equal score is not as great as a win, but it is far better than losing!

They all pat Mark on the back. "Thanks for helping us out, man. You're welcome to join us any time again." Mark looks tired. Tired but happy. Very happy.

"Thanks for giving Mark an opportunity to play, Coach. This has been one of the most exciting days of his life," Mark's dad was saying. "You know, he hasn't had much fun in his life. Feeding him and dressing him take up so much time, because he can't do it independently, so there is not much time left for doing the fun things and as he doesn't have friends coming over to visit him, he mostly just sits in front of the TV and watches football."

Daniel was listening to all of this. "What happened to Mark? Why is he in the wheelchair?" All these questions seemed to just pour out of Daniel's mouth.

"Mark has cerebral palsy, CP for short. In his case that means that before he was even born, a part of his brain, the part that stores all the information about your muscles and how they work, didn't develop the same as other children's. It is not something that somebody did wrong and it's nobody's fault."

"Does that mean that Mark's muscles don't work together and tell him how to walk?"

"Exactly, but even more than that, that is why he has problems keeping his head up, and why his arms are stiff and seem to flap about. That also makes it difficult for Mark to speak clearly. You can understand some of the words he says, but that is why they are also teaching him to read at school, so that he might be able to use a computer to speak for him one day. His family understands most of what he says but it is very difficult for other people to chat to him."

"I didn't think Mark would be able to read." Daniel was being honest. He thought that if Mark's brain wasn't telling his muscles how to walk and talk, the brain wouldn't be able to tell Mark how to read.

"You're half right and half wrong, young man," Mark's dad was saying. "Some people with CP have no problems with reading and writing and some do have problems. Just like the fact that some people with CP have stiff muscles which makes their arms and legs so straight, some are floppy and that is why their heads hang and some have a bit of both, like Mark."

"Can't they operate on him so that he will be able to walk?" Daniel was thinking about the old lady who lives close to them and who had a hip operation. After the operation she was able to walk again.

"No, unfortunately they can't," said Mark's dad.

Out of the corner of his eye, Daniel was seeing his own dad approach. "Guess it's time to go. Thanks for playing in our team, Mark. You kicked that ball at exactly the right moment! I'll see you around."

Mark looked Daniel in the eye and smiled, nodding his head. His dad hugged him. "This is the most fun we've ever had at football," he was saying.

Mark was still smiling, nodding his head. "I told you that we should persevere and attend every match, didn't I? See, it paid off. We'll be back next Saturday, and I don't know about you, but I think you've gotten yourself a friend at school, too."

And if you look closely, you can see how proud Mark's dad is. His son had saved the day for the Wimbledon football club.

Activities for 6 to 8 year olds

Mark's feelings

In Circle Time ask the children to think about times they have been left out of things for some reason. Ask volunteers to say what happened and how they felt.

Ask them to think about how Mark felt at the football, always watching.

Ask each child in turn to give you one word to say how they think he felt. (Those who repeat a word can change places with the child who said it last.)

Ask the children to finish the sentence:

'When Mark joined in and scored a goal I think he felt…'

Collect these feelings words and put them alongside the others making two lists they can use in their writing.

At first, Mark felt…

sad
wishing he could play
out of things
not allowed
different
it was unfair

Then he felt…

great
happy
was joining in
like everyone else

Wheels experience

If you have someone in your class who has a wheelchair, ask their parent/carer if you can borrow it for this activity. Otherwise, perhaps social services, the Red Cross or the school nurse could obtain one for you to use.

Either ask your wheelchair bound pupil to tell the children how it works – this will differ from chair to chair depending on how sophisticated it is – or sit yourself in the chair and explain its functions.

Explain to the children that you want them to experience how it feels to be in a wheelchair and that each group will have the chair for one work session. Ask each child to spend a minute in the chair to control it and then in turn to sit in their chair as they work.

It could be too time consuming for each child to experience a playtime in the chair, but perhaps you could incorporate it into a PE session either outdoors or in the hall.

At the end of the wheelchair experience, ask each child to draw or write an account of how they felt when they were wheelchair bound. Ask how they felt sitting down and always having to look up at other people. Ask the children to think up some slogans to help wheelchair bound children to feel better about being in their chair.

Activities for 9 to 11 year olds

Daniel's feelings

In Circle Time, remind the children that it was Daniel who suggested that Mark should be allowed in the team. Ask volunteers to say how they think Daniel felt when Mark scored a goal.

Ask children to think about what they could do to make a child in a wheelchair feel included in class activities and ask them to finish the sentence:

'If I knew someone in a wheelchair I could...'

Paralympics

In Circle Time talk about the Olympic Games and the people who train for these games for many years. Ask the children to tell you what they know about them.

Explain that there are also games for people with disabilities so that they can compete on an equal footing against others who have disabilities.

I could...

- include him in my games
- talk to him
- walk by their wheelchair into lessons
- make sure he doesn't feel left out
- think about his feelings
- help other people to understand how it feels
- talk about what interests him
- invite him home and to parties

Explain about the Stoke Mandeville Games which were organised after the Second World War to help with the rehabilitation of World War II veterans suffering from spinal injuries. These first games in 1948 grew into the Paralympics. Field events are discus, javelin, shot, high jump and long jump. Sports and games include archery, basketball, boccia, bowling, cycling, equestrian events, fencing, goalball, judo, football, shooting, swimming, table tennis, tennis, volleyball and weight/power lifting.

Winter paralympics were first held in 1976 and events included Alpine and Nordic skiing, ice-sledge hockey and ice-sledge racing.

Start a long-term project with the children, asking them to find out all they can about these games, both locally and nationally. Ask them to look in local and national newspapers, watch TV, use encyclopaedias and the internet. Explain that you will prepare a notice-board for their contributions.

Try and find someone in your community who is paraplegic who would be willing to come into school and talk about his or her way of life and whether they play any form of sport.

Share the children's research with others in the school – children, teachers, governors and health professionals.

Magic Moments at Burger Bite

2. Magic Moments at Burger Bite

Information

This story is about a child meeting a young woman with Down's syndrome in Burger Bite*, becoming curious about her and wanting to know about the condition. Reflection on the story and the suggested activities will help children to understand and accept Hannah's condition with empathy and understanding.

Some schools meeting a young person with Down's syndrome will be doing so for the first time but those who may have had a Down's child previously should not expect the young person to have the same kind of personality. Many think that all children with Down's syndrome have extremely happy personalities, but this is not always true. These children have as varied personalities as others; they are all unique individuals and should be acknowledged as a person first and foremost.

It was once thought that there were many things that people with Down's syndrome could not do when in fact they had never been given the opportunity to try. Much of the knowledge that children acquire naturally, for example, making purchases, interacting with others, caring for oneself, needs to be taught to Down's children. Today opportunities are greater and many people with Down's syndrome lead rich and varied lives.

Normally an early intervention programme will be in place for a Down's child.

Down's syndrome is named after Dr. John L H Down, English physician (1828-1896) who first officially described the condition.

Down's syndrome:

▸ is caused by a chromosome abnormality by the representation of chromosome 21 three times, instead of twice, in some or all cells

▸ is also called chromosome 21-trisomy syndrome or mongolism

▸ occurs approximately once in every 700 births and across all ethnic groups

▸ is often recognised by what is called a 'mongoloid' look to the face, with a short nose, Asian-looking eyes and small ears set low on the head

▸ has a wide variety of symptoms and is characterised by varying degrees of hearing loss and speech impairment, as well as other physical signs, such as a thick tongue, extra eyelid folds and short, stubby fingers

▸ can present up to 120 characteristics; most children have no more than six or seven of these

▸ children may also experience cognitive problems, including mental retardation and problems with physical co-ordination.

The Down's syndrome Association (DSA) 12-13 Clapham Common South Side, London, SW4 7AA, offers an 'Education Support Pack for Schools' with simple information sheets on specific topics.

Useful books include:

Down Syndrome, The Facts, Mark Selikowitz, OUP 1990 (Some authorities use the term 'Down Syndrome'.)

There are many websites:

www.dsa-uk.com

www.downsnet.org

* The choice of a burger bar as an eating blace for a 'treat meal' does not imply that the authors wish to promote this type of food for frequent consumption.

Note: Activities for 9 to 11 year olds. In these activities, issues about inherited characteristics are discussed. If you have a looked after child in your class it may be helpful to discuss this activity with them before hand as they may not have the knowledge to participate in this activity.

Magic Moments at Burger Bite

The young woman approached the table and asked, "Have you finished?" James looked up. His mum had brought him to Burger Bite for a reward, because he had managed to keep his room tidy for a whole week.

"Not quite," Mrs Green smiled. James also smiled. He had just had a his favourite meal. Life couldn't get much better than this.

When the young Burger Bite worker moved out of hearing distance, James leaned over to his mum and whispered, "Mum, did you see that the girl who asked about clearing the table looks a bit different? Her eyes look different and her hands too. She also talked funny."

"Yes, I saw. She looks different because she has Down's syndrome."

"Down's syndrome? What's that?" James asked taking a large gulp of his drink.

"I'm not exactly sure," Mrs Green replied, "but it has something to do with chromosomes."

"What are chromosomes?"

"You know that your whole body is made up of little cells, don't you? If you scratch your skin, many of these little cells come off. Chromosomes are the things that are inside these cells."

Just then the young woman came back. "Can I take the trays now?"

"Yes, thank you." Mrs Green and James smiled at her, and their smiles were met by the broadest, friendliest smile they had seen in a long time.

"It looks like you're busy today," Mrs Green said.

"Yes it is busy," said the woman. "It's better when it's busy. I have to do more things and I meet new people."

James, curious, asked, "What's your name?"

"My name is Hannah," said the girl pointing to her name badge.

"I'm James," replied James, now a little shy. They looked at each other with smiles.

"Well, we'd best be off now," said Mrs Green as her and James stood up. "We'll see you soon though Hannah. It was lovely meeting you."

"Bye!" said Hannah with a wave. "See you soon!"

Outside Burger Bite, Mum told James that Burger Bite were good to their workers and were especially happy to employ people with disabilities.

"That's good for Hannah," said James. Then he said, "Mum, you were talking about chromosomes and Down's syndrome. How do the chromosomes work?"

"I don't know much more, I'm afraid. I just know that people with Down's syndrome have a different number of chromosomes." They walked in silence for a little while.

"I know, why don't we look on the Web? I'm sure we'll find something there!" said James.

Mrs Green ruffled James' hair. "Yes, that's a great idea, my little want-to-know-it all."

James looked intently as his mum typed the word "Down's syndrome" into the search engine. Before long a blue screen appeared. "What does it say? Read it, Mum, read!" James' curiosity made him almost impatient.

"Down's syndrome, or Trisomy 21 is characterised by having three, rather than two copies of chromosome 21 in each cell," Mrs Green read.

"Mum, there's that word, chromosome again. What does that mean?" Mrs Green glanced at the page. "Let me see. Mmmm. Basically it says that chromosomes work almost like the motherboard of your computer. The chromosomes are the little cells that carry all the information about you. It has information about the colour of your eyes and the colour of your hair. Even about the size of your feet! Now, children with Down's syndrome have this extra chromosome and that chromosome also carries certain information about the way they look, and what they do."

"Is that why Hannah's hands and eyes look different?"

"Yes, but let's see, there is a whole list of typical characteristics of people with Down's syndrome. Individuals with Down's syndrome are usually characterised by a short stature (that means they aren't very tall), have eyes that slant upward with folds at the inner corner, have small ears with small ear canals, a small mouth with a high and sharp palate, a broad neck with excessive skin about it and small hands and feet. Some people with Down's syndrome have a single crease across the hand palm and shorter fingers."

"That sounds exactly like Hannah! What else do they say?"

"They also say that people with Down's syndrome think a bit more slowly, which means that they have to work hard to learn to do things like reading and writing, crossing a street, climbing stairs and catching a ball. They also take longer to learn to talk and that is why they often use short sentences. Their chromosomes give their body a message that they look a bit different, talk a bit different and think a bit different.

People with Down's syndrome are also often jovial and like interacting with people. However, this is not always the case, and some individuals might shun other people and enjoy being left alone."

"I guess that is just like us, all the children in my class are not the same. Some are friendlier than others and some get angry very quickly. And they don't have Down's syndrome."

"That's exactly it, James. People with Down's syndrome don't all fit into the same box. These things that are written about them and the way they look and behave are just to make it easier for us to understand them. We can't put them in a box and say all people with Down's syndrome are exactly the same. People with Down's syndrome, like all other people, look like their parents, like the same things the family like and often have the same talents as the other family members. Therefore they all different from one another just as you are different from your friends at school."

James suddenly frowned. "Why does Hannah have Down's syndrome? What makes it happen?"

Mrs Green clicked on an icon and started reading. "It says here that they are not sure what causes it, but it is something they are born with. It is not anybody's fault that it happens and it cannot be changed or cured. It is just one of those things one has to accept."

"Mum, I think we need to print all of this and tomorrow I'm going to tell everyone about our trip to Burger Bite and how I met Hannah."

Activities for 6 to 8 year olds

I remember...

Burger Bite Burger Meal 10

being different 4

being the same 3

Hannah's Job 8

nobody's fault 1

usually happy people 2

Which bit of the story do you remember?

In Circle Time, after you have read the story, ask all the children to close their eyes for a moment and think about the part of the story that they remember best. Ask the children to finish this sentence:

'I remember the bit about...'

Jot down the children's responses and the numbers of children who remember each part.

Now ask the children to think about the most important part of the story – is there a message there that everyone can understand? Ask them to finish the sentence:

'The message in this story is...' Ask children who repeat someone's answer to change places.

Same and different

Ask the children to think about how the children in your class are all the same. Ask them to finish the sentence:

'We are all the same because we all have...'

Ask the children to think about how all the children in your class are different and to finish the sentence:

'I am different because I...'

Talk with the children about how Down's children are the same and also how they are different from each other.

Remind the children that it is polite and well mannered not to stare at people they meet who look a little different from them. Remind them also about how James treated Hannah as his equal, he was interested and polite but didn't make Hannah feel uncomfortable. Ask them to draw a picture of themselves doing something that would help a Down's syndrome child feel good about himself. Use the pictures to make a display to share with others in the school. Ask children to choose the title.

Activities for 9 to 11 year olds

Chromosones

Ask the children to say this word. Write it up so that they can see how it looks.

Talk with the children about the numbers of chromosomes we all have – 23 pairs and that half of these come from our fathers and half from our mothers.

Ask the children to raise a hand if they can tell you how many chromosomes there are in 23 pairs. As Down's syndrome children have an extra chromosome 21 – how many chromosomes do they have altogether?

Talk about inherited characteristics and how we are made from half our mother and half our father. Ask the children to think about the characteristics they have from one parent or the other.

Ask them to finish this sentence:

'One of my characteristics is…and I get it from my…

From my mother I get my brown hair and blue eyes. From my dad I get my height and my colouring.

Remind the children that we are each different and special and that even though our brothers and sisters get the same number of chromosomes from each parent, no two brothers or sisters are identical.

Remind them that Down's syndrome children are also different from each other.

We are all equal

In Circle Time talk to the children about how all humans have the same general characteristics, but that we are all unique and special. Explain that children who do not have Down's syndrome have many advantages over children who do and that there are many employments that are not suitable for people with Down's.

Ask each child to finish these sentences, either orally in Circle Time or in writing:

'If I had Down's I would feel…'

'If I had Down's I would want people to…'

Explain to the children that there are some companies that have a policy to employ people with conditions such as Down's and that this policy is to be commended.

Remind the children that it is polite and well mannered not to stare at people they meet who look a little different from them. Remind them also about how James treated Hannah as his equal, he was interested and polite and didn't make Hannah feel uncomfortable.

Kyle and the Hairdresser

3. Kyle and the Hairdresser

Information

The following story is about a child and an adult who both have dyslexia; how they feel about it and what the adult had to do to overcome the difficulties. It may help children to understand dyslexia and recognise with empathy the difficulties and restrictions that dyslexic children in school have to overcome.

The word 'dyslexia' comes from the Greek and means 'difficulty with words'. In dyslexic people there is a difference in the brain area that deals with language, affecting the underlying skills needed in order to read, write and spell. Brain imaging techniques show that dyslexic people process information differently.

Dyslexia covers a broad range of difficulties associated with literacy and learning, particularly written language; it sometimes includes mathematical and musical notation.

'It is estimated that 10% of the population suffers from dyslexia to some extent and that about four people in every hundred need special help.'

(Dyslexia, How would I cope, p16.)

There may be several causes and each dyslexic person is different. Many, but not all, dyslexic people have special talents and positive abilities.

Dyslexia may also present as a difficulty in:

- speed of processing
- organising
- short-term memory
- sequencing
- auditory/visual perception
- spoken language
- word finding
- motor skills.

Useful books include:

Ostler, C. (1994) *Dyslexia, a parents' survival guide*, Ammonite books, Godalming UK.

Ryden, Michael (1992) *Dyslexia, How would I cope?* Jessica Kingsley Publications, London.

The Dyslexia Association, 98 London Road, Reading, RG1 5AU publishes an annual handbook.

There are many useful websites including:

www.bda-dyslexia.org.uk

www.dyslexic.com

Kyle and the Hairdresser

Kyle was looking at the mirror very intently while the hairdresser was combing his hair. It felt as if she was too close to him and he was aware of every single hair on his head.

"So, how is school these days?" She tried to strike up a conversation, but had picked a sensitive topic.

"Oh, I don't like school that much," Kyle said. The hairdresser's interest was sparked, because she had never enjoyed school herself. "How come you don't like school? Is it the other kids in your class? Or the teacher?"

"It's lots of things," Kyle replied. "My mum explained to me that I have dyslexia. It is a complicated sort of language problem, which makes reading and writing difficult for me and at school that's all you do the whole time – read and write. Read and write. Until it comes out of your ears! It's not that I don't like books, but, reading is difficult for me and I don't like doing things that I'm not so good at."

"Well Kyle, can you believe it? I had exactly the same problem. When I was still at school, the teachers used to think that I was either stupid or that I was being very lazy. They thought that if they punished me enough, they would eventually get me to read…Of course that didn't help. It only made me resent school even more and it also make me scared of the teacher. When I didn't understand something, I was too sacred to put up my hand and ask. I still remember how often I was in trouble because I kept on forgetting to take my homework books to school or I would forget to take them home. That meant that I had double trouble, from my mum and from the teacher!"

"I know how you feel," Kyle said. "Sometimes I take the whole evening to do my homework and then I still forget to take it with me to school. That makes me so angry with myself! In class my teacher chose a buddy for me. His name is Liam. He sits next to me and checks that I write down my homework in my diary and that I remember to pack my diary into my bag. He also helps me to tidy my work tray where I keep my books at the end of the day so that it looks just as neat at the others kid's trays. It's not like he's bossy or anything – he just says 'Hey, let's check our bags' and we do it together."

"Wow! That's one kind teacher you have. You are very lucky! One of the other things I also remember very clearly," the hairdresser continued, "was that I could never sit still in class. The teacher sometimes even tied me to the chair, but that made me want to move even more and then I would always get detention because I was disrupting the whole class."

"Actually, my teacher is very understanding," Kyle said. "When I start wriggling, she just winks at me which is a sign that she understands and if I can't sit still any longer, then she sends me on an errand so that I can take a message to another teacher. Getting out of the classroom for a little while really helps a lot. And the other kids don't know – that is the best.

My teacher said that I must pretend that I have an imaginary hoop around me. That helps me to not stand or sit too close to people and it also helps people not to be too close to me, because I don't like it when people are too close. That creates our own little space. We call it 'our hoop space'. And when we sit on the carpet for Circle Time, we sit cross-legged and our knees don't touch, because we all sit in our own imaginary hoop. My teacher also says that we are only allowed to use our hands to help each other and not hurt each other. That way, we don't get annoyed with each other and fight."

"That sounds like you have a really great teacher," the hairdresser said, meaning every word.

"There are lots of other things she does." Kyle was remembering. "When we have group work, she never asks me to be the scribe, but I get to do the report back. And when the other kids have say 20 sums to do, I only have to do 5, but they are the most difficult five, because I'm good at maths. She also gives me extra time to write things down. I do exactly the same work as the other kids, but I get to write fewer words. And the best of all is that the teacher arranged for me to do some of the tests by talking instead of writing. That really helps a lot!"

"How things have changed!" the hairdresser exclaimed. "And when you're grown-up, what do you want to do then?" the hairdresser was inquisitive.

"I've figured it all out. I want to be an engineer. Just like my dad. And guess what? He also has dyslexia and it hasn't stopped him!"

The hairdresser gently squeezed Kyle's shoulder. "You're a special kid, do you know that?"

"No, I don't think so. I'm just an ordinary dyslexic boy, but one with great plans. And, by the way, I really like the way you cut my hair. I think it looks kind of cool."

Activities for 6 to 8 year olds

Kyle's feelings

In Circle Time talk about how it is difficult for dyslexic children to read and write. Explain that it is not the child's fault, but that it is something in their brain that is not wired the same as other children's. Explain that sometimes dyslexic children have other gifts and find other work easy to understand.

Kyle could feel:

thick

sad

slow

unhappy

hot and bothered

He wants to give up.

He wants to speak not write.

He'd say 'please tell me, don't make me read it.'

Ask the children to think about how it must feel to be unable to write their names. Can they remember how they learnt to write it? Ask volunteers to tell you their memories of learning to write their name. Explain that if they can't remember, it usually means that they had no difficulty in writing it.

Do the above activity with reading.

Now ask the children to think about how Kyle would feel if he kept trying and trying to write his name and it didn't come right. Ask volunteers to tell you words or phrases to describe these feelings. Make a list and talk about the words the children have given you.

Ask the children to close their eyes and think about feeling like this and how much worse it would be if people shouted at you or said you were stupid because you couldn't do it.

Talk about what they could do to make a dyslexic child feel better about her work.

Difficult writing

Ask each child to write their name. Now ask them to put their pencil in the wrong (for them) hand and to write their name underneath the first writing.

Can they see the difference – how do they feel about writing with the wrong hand?

Ask them to think about:

▸ how they would feel if their work was untidy even when they treid really hard

▸ how their teachers or parents/carers would feel.

Now ask them to think how they would feel if other people were unkind about their work – if they mocked it or laughed about it.

Ask them to hold their pencil in the correct hand and to write a sentence about how they would feel if people were unkind about their work. Ask them to write another sentence about what they could do to help a dyslexic child feel better about his work.

Activities for 9 to 11 year old children

Difficult reading

Prepare a sheet for each child with two or three simple sentences with symbols and numbers in between each letter. <u>There is a sheet in the back of the book that you can photocopy.</u>

Make this a fun session and tell the children that today they are going to read some unusual writing with a symbol in between each letter. Ask for a volunteer to read the first sentence on their paper. Ask various children to do the same with the other sentences.

I l=i4v£e i%n t*h+i&s t*o"wln.

l6t i"s h)ot t*o&d%a£y.

I l%i&k$e r%e"a!d*i&n)g.

Ask children to work in pairs, each to write a simple sentence with a symbol in between each letter, exchange papers and read them to the other child. They could use timers to see how long it takes them to 'read' the sentences.

Ask the children to work in pairs to try to mirror-write a simple sentence. Can their partner read it?

Then talk with the children about their difficulty in reading what they don't know and explain that this is exactly what children who are dyslexic have to try to do.

Codes and de-coding

Ask the children to write a letter replacement code; a=b, b=c, c=d ... You might need to have the alphabet displayed somewhere in the classroom. Now ask them to write their name, using the code. Collect, mix up and re-distribute the papers and ask each child to read out the correct name written down on their paper. Make this a fun session by pretending to be impatient – and asking the children to be quick about their 'reading'.

Extend this activity by asking the children to work in pairs, each to write something about themselves and the other to de-code it. You could ask them to devise a new code.

After this session, talk seriously with the children about the difficulties that some children, especially those who are dyslexic, have with reading and writing.Can they see that being impatient or unkind can hurt children's feelings, especially if they have been trying hard to get it right?

Can they themselves do anything to help children who have difficulties with their work to feel better about it?

Solution:

I live in this town. It is hot today. I like reading.

Toni and the Boy who was Different

4. Toni and the Boy who was Different

Information

This story is about Joss, who is autistic. This condition is more recognised in schools these days and the children will probably have met children such as Joss. It is hoped that through the story the children will be able recognise Joss's difficulties and relate to him with understanding and empathy.

Autism is a condition that affects the way a person communicates and relates to those around them. Children and adults with autism have difficulties with everyday social interaction. Their capacity to understand other people's emotional expressions makes it difficult for them to develop friendships. Because those with autism are not physically disabled and look just like anyone else, it makes it much harder to create awareness and understanding of the condition. An autistic person finds the world to be a bewildering or frightening place.

People with autism can often have accompanying learning disabilities but everyone with the condition shares a difficulty in making sense of the world.

In Great Britain over 200,000 people of all ages have disorders in the autistic spectrum.

Autism is characterised by:

> ‣ impairments of social interaction, appearing aloof or indifferent to others

> ‣ inappropriate behaviour

> ‣ difficulties in communication with little eye contact

> ‣ inability to use imagination

> ‣ resistance to change

> ‣ limited and repetitive pattern of activity

> ‣ inability to learn from social interaction or to make sense of experiences.

Thus the autistic child needs:

> ‣ an organised structured environment

> ‣ an organised structured teaching programme

> ‣ a daily routine.

Useful books include:

Wing, Lorna (1996) *The Autistic Spectrum, A guide for parents and professionals*, Constable, London.

There are many websites including:

www.nas.org.uk

www.autismconnect.org

www.autism.org

www.autism-awareness.org.uk

Toni and the Boy who was Different

Toni was very excited and in a hurry to go home, but the school day seemed to go on for ever. Her mummy had just had a baby so her granny was visiting to help with Toni and the new family member.

The smell of freshly baked muffins hung in the air as Toni opened the door and heard her Granny's loving, welcoming words. "Hello dear. I have a lovely surprise for you."

"Muffins!" Toni exclaimed and couldn't wait to sink her teeth into one of her granny's delicious soft muffins. She was very happy to have a granny who cared about her so much.

"You know, Gran," Toni said when she finally paused between two mouthfuls, "we have a new boy in class. His name is Joss. He is really strange. He doesn't want to talk to us or play with us. He wanders around on the playground all by himself and sometimes he starts flapping his hands and then he looks at them very closely. Sometimes when the teacher talks to him, he repeats her words. Like today, when Mrs Edwards said, "You have to sit now," he repeated, "You have to sit now" in exactly the same way! It was so funny and we all laughed, but Mrs Edwards didn't think it was funny. She told us to stop laughing immediately and to carry on with our work."

While Toni was happily chatting away, her granny listened with a gentle smile. "Toni, my dear, you must remember that we are all different. Think of the different birds. They don't all look alike, and they don't all sing alike. Some are brightly coloured, some are dull. Some have hoarse voices like the beautiful peacock and some sing sweetly like the dull lark. Don't treat Joss as different; treat him like one of your friends."

Toni thought about this for some time and decided that she would explain it to her friends the next day and try and make friends with Joss.

The next day Toni did her best to make friends with Joss, while all her friends watched. But it was no use! He just sat in the classroom, rocking to and fro, while spinning a rubber that he found somewhere in the classroom, around and around and around. Toni felt that he didn't even notice her and that he definitely didn't want to talk to her.

She told her Granny all about this strange behaviour and then Granny said. "You have to remember that we are all different. Think of the different crayons in your pencil case. Some are sharp, some are dull, some are pretty, and they all have different colours. But the important thing is that they all have to live together in your pencil case. Think about that when you see Joss tomorrow."

Toni really wanted to understand Joss and be his friend, because she saw that her other friends laughed when Joss behaved in a weird way or when he repeated everything that Mrs Edwards said. It looked as if their laughing didn't matter to Joss but Toni felt sad.

What a wonderful day waited for Toni and her friends when they arrived at school the next day. Mrs Edwards had planned a visit to the zoo. Everybody was happy, but Joss threw a huge tantrum. When they eventually got to the zoo, he started enjoying himself.

Toni couldn't wait to tell Granny all the news. "We had such a wonderful time, Granny! And Joss was so clever; he knew exactly where we had to walk to get to the penguins. When we got there, he started talking about all the different types and how they differ from each other and what they eat and how many eggs they lay – too many things to remember! He really knows a lot about penguins. He even knew that there is a street called Penguin Boulevard in America!"

"Joss might not know what to do with a rubber, but he seems to know a lot about penguins! Some people are especially interested in one particular subject and they concentrate all their interest into that."

As usual the next school day started with everybody on the carpet gathered around Mrs Edwards for Circle Time. They sang a welcome song. They spoke about the weather. They told their news. Then Toni saw that Joss wasn't there. Mrs Edwards must have noticed this too, because she said, "As you all know, we have a new friend in class – Joss. I am also sure that you noticed that Joss behaves in a different way. That is because he has autism. Autism means that Joss is not always aware of what is happening in the world around him and that it seems to us as if he lives in a world of his own. A world we don't always understand."

Toni was fascinated and she wanted to hear more. Mrs Edwards continued. "That means that he has three great difficulties. The first difficulty is with talking. That means that he battles to tell us what he wants and what he likes. It also means that it is difficult for him to always understand what we are trying to tell him. Have you noticed that when we call him, he doesn't always respond to his name?" A few of the children nodded.

"His second difficulty is with making and keeping friends. This is not because he doesn't want friends, but he doesn't understand all the rules of friendship. Sometimes things interest him more than a friend would. I wonder if you've seen how he spins the eraser around and around, or how he plays with a piece of string?"

The children on the carpet were fascinated and listened with big eyes, and Mrs Edwards continued, "Joss's daddy told me that he likes chasing games and he enjoys it when he can run around and you chase him. But he doesn't understand that he also needs to chase you back and therefore you will have to teach him that." Toni started smiling because she now knew how she could start involving Joss on the playground.

"Joss's third difficulty is that he has very specific routines as he needs order and predictability to feel safe. I am sure you have all noticed how he always opens his lunchbox and then unpacks everything in a neat row from the biggest to the smallest with exactly the same spaces between everything before he starts to eat. And when he eventually starts eating, he smells everything first."

"My mum says it is rude to smell food," said Jonny.

"Yes, Jonny, your mum is quite right, but Joss doesn't smell the food to be rude. If you want to make sure that you have cheese and jam on your sandwich, you look to see, but Joss uses his sense of smell to find out what he has on his sandwich. He also eats in the same way. I have noticed that he always starts with his sandwiches before he has his apple and his juice."

"Mmm, is that why he always has cheese on his sandwich and a red apple?" Sarah chirped before Jamie said, "Yes, and I saw that he always has orange juice!"

Mrs Edwards smiled because she saw that they were beginning to understand what it meant to have autism. "Yes, Joss thinks that juice should always be orange. Toni, can you still remember how Joss cried when you tried to share your green cold drink with him? That is because he thinks everything that one drinks should be orange." This made Toni feel better.

"But you all have to realise that this doesn't mean that Joss is stupid although it might take him longer to learn certain things. There are some things that he is very good at, like yesterday with the penguins, so I don't want you to laugh at Joss or bully him."

Toni felt happy. "My Granny told me that we are all different, like the birds or like our crayons," she explained to the others. "If we wanted to make a beautiful picture, we couldn't leave out one of the colours – we have to use them all. Even if Joss is different and does things we don't understand, he can still be our friend."

Activities for 6 to 8 year olds

Joss's difficulties

In Circle Time talk about how Joss is different from other children in the class. Write up the words 'autistic' and 'autism'. Ask the children if they know anyone who is autistic and if so ask them to tell the group about them.

> **Joss knew about:**
>
> different kinds of penguins
>
> where they were in the zoo
>
> the eggs they lay
>
> what they eat

Ask the children to think about how Joss is the same as all the other boys in the class. Ask them to finish the sentence:

'Joss is the same because…'

Now ask the children to think about how Joss is different from other children in the class. Ask volunteers to tell you what Joss told the children on the visit to the zoo. Ask them to finish the sentence:

'Joss told them…'

Ask children to think about the three great difficulties that Joss has and write these down on the chalkboard or flip-chart.

Talk about the difficulty that Joss has with talking. Ask volunteers to say how they think they would feel if they couldn't easily say what they wanted to say. Talk about the words the children give you and explain what they mean to the others in the class.

Ask the children to think about what they could do to help someone like Joss to feel better about himself. Talk about their responsibility to look after all children and not make it harder by being unkind or laughing when they do something which seems unusual.

Smells

Prepare some covered food items for the children to identify by smell. Make a game of it by having pencil and paper near the numbered items and asking the children to visit the table and to draw what they think each smell is. Make sure that no-one peeks; or you could blindfold the children!

In Circle Time ask the children to tell you what they think the smells are and write up their suggestions and the numbers of children who got each one correct. Ask which was the easiest food to identify and which was the hardest.

Remind them that in the story Joss had to use his sense of smell to identify what he was eating for lunch.

Activities for 9 to 11 year olds

The first activity for 6-8 year olds is also suitable for older children.

Joss's difficulties

In Circle Time ask the children to think about the difficulties that Joss would have in school because of his autism.

Ask them to finish the sentence:

'Joss could have difficulty because…'

Ask volunteers to say what they could do to help Joss if he were in their class.

Talk about Joss wanting food to be certain colours. Ask children to work in pairs, choose one colour and then think up a menu for a meal with all the food in that one colour. Come together in Circle Time to talk about their menus. Ask volunteers to tell you what they think about only eating foods or drinking drinks in certain colours and how difficult it must be for Joss's family to make his meals. Use the words 'restricted diet' and ask the children to tell you the meaning.

I could…

be a good friend

sit by him in class

choose to play with him

make sure no-one is unkind to him

include him in games

ask him about his interests

understand his difficulties

Routines

Spontaneous means:

unplanned

unprompted

impulsive

spur of the moment

unstructured

Talk with the children about Joss's need for routine. Ask them to think about their morning routine and ask volunteers to say what they do each morning before they come to school.

Ask the children whether they have other routines, such as the shops they visit, their bedtime routine – are these always the same?

Talk about spontaneous activities as being the opposite from routine. Can they give you other words that mean this?

Ask them to give some examples of spontaneity in your classroom? Can they tell you about spontaneous happenings at home or on holiday?

Ask them to make two columns on a piece of paper and to give each a heading – routine, spontaneous. Ask them to write in each column three things they like to do and then to write underneath a definition of spontaneous and routine. Ask them to write a few sentences about being spontaneous and having a routine and the benefits of both.

My Sister, Chantelle

5. My Sister, Chantelle

Information

In this story Ashley's sister Chantelle is blind. Many children may not have met partially sighted children in school and this story gives an opportunity for them to recognise the difficulties that such children and adults face in the outside world. Ashley is rightly proud of her sister's achievements and as she highlights these, your children will come to understand that, with help and apparatus such people can live a near normal life.

You may find the following information about blindness useful.

▸ Blindness may be caused by heredity, accident or disease.

▸ A hereditary disease, called retinitis pigmentosa is a common cause of blindness which affects 1.2 million people worldwide.

▸ Education of the blind was begun by Valentin Haüy, who published a book with raised lettering in 1784 and founded a school.

▸ Aids to the blind include the use of the Braille and Moon alphabets in reading and writing.

▸ Guide dogs for the blind were first trained in Germany for soldiers blinded in World War I.

▸ In the UK 17,000 people with sight problems use a white cane. Another 5,000 use guide dogs. There are many more who need help with their everyday living.

RNIB works to enable people with sight problems to live their daily lives independently. It offers magazines and books in Braille and has a talking book service.

More Information

RNIB Helpline on 0845 766 9999 for a wide range of information about sight loss.

Useful websites include:

www.omni.ac.uk

www.rnib.org.uk/xpedio/groups/public/documents/PublicWebsite/

The above site has details of short courses on subjects such as legislation, literacy, music and maths and accredited training programmes for learning support assistants and teachers.

LINKS

▸ Ask the children to look out for references to blind or partially
   sighted people in newspapers, TV or sports and make a class book
   or wall display about them and celebrate their achievements.

▸ Invite a blind person with their guide dog to come and talk to the children.

▸ Find out about puppy walkers.

My Sister, Chantelle

Ashley stood up in front of the whole class. It was her turn to tell her friends all about somebody in her family.

"I want to tell you about my younger sister. Her name is Chantelle." Ashley's eyes always lit up when she spoke about Chantelle. She had decided that she was the family member she wanted to talk about in Circle Time. "She is very smart and can do all kinds of things. She likes to play, but she doesn't like plastic toys much, she prefers real things, like a real hammer and not a plastic one, because the plastic one doesn't have the same weight or shape and it doesn't make the same sound when you bang it! She can be very funny and likes to make us laugh. When Mummy gives her something to eat and she doesn't tell her what it is, she pulls funny faces trying to decide what she is eating. That is because she is blind."

Now all the other children were listening wide-eyed. "When I was 5 and she was 3 we had a terrible car crash. I broke my arm; can you still see the scar?"

Ashley pulled up the sleeve of her jersey slightly. "Well after that, Chantelle was blind. She has a type of blindness called cortical blindness. That means that her eyes can actually see, but that her brain can't understand what it sees and therefore she's actually blind. There are also other reasons why some people are blind. Some are born blind, some have diseases of the eye and some have accidents like Chantelle had. Blindness is not something that you can 'catch' like a cold or like mumps, so you don't have to be scared to play with blind children."

Ashley was in her element now. She enjoyed being a teacher and telling the other children about blindness.

"In our house we have had to make certain changes to help Chantelle find her way about. Just after the accident, the doctor said that it is very important that we don't feel sorry for her or start doing everything for her. We have to help her do things as independently as possible. One of the first things our mummy did was to put a string of bells round the handle of her bedroom door. That helped her find her room easily, because every time she pushed the door open she heard the bells jingling. In the beginning it was difficult for Chantelle to learn to walk again, because it is quite scary finding your way about when you can't see. She had a wooden trolley that she would push that helped her to orientate. It helped know that the floor was beneath her feet and the ceiling was above her. This was also safer, because every time she banged into the wall, she banged with the trolley and didn't hurt herself. Sometimes we gave her a backpack put on back to front with heavy things in it, so that she didn't feel as if she was floating in the sky. This also freed her hands so she could feel her way around. She still doesn't like going on her tricycle or on the swing because she likes her feet being on the ground.

"Getting her to eat again was quite a problem! She was scared to just open her mouth and to let us feed her. Imagine closing your eyes so that you can't see and people just sticking things into your mouth." A slight shudder went through some of Ashley's classroom friends.

"The therapist said we have to always tell Chantelle what we are putting in her mouth. She also used to sniff and smell all the food, which made Mummy really, really angry as she said it was bad manners, until the therapist explained that it was her way of finding out what the food was. These days she doesn't sniff the food so obviously, but does it very quickly as her general sense of smell is well developed now. She has also started eating all by herself. Dad just cuts her meat and we have to always put the meat at the top of the plate and then tell her that the rice is on the right hand side, the peas at the bottom and the beans on the left. That helps her to not be too messy at the table and to find her food."

"Her teacher has also made some changes in the classroom for her. There is a blind by the window where she sits, so that when the sunlight shines through, it doesn't bother her. She also uses a light box with shapes on it, because the difference between light and dark helps her find things more easily. During Circle Time when they talk about something, her teacher will always give her something to hold, because that helps her to make a picture in her head. Like when they spoke about the police, she gave her a real policeman's hat. It doesn't help to give her a plastic toy policeman, because if you have your eyes closed and you feel it, it doesn't feel like anything near a MAN at all – it's just a hard plastic thing."

"In the beginning we didn't like to go out with Chantelle, because people stared at us. Maybe they were feeling sorry for her. Maybe they were curious. Maybe they wondered what was wrong with her. Maybe they thought she was stupid because sometimes she would poke at her eyes and suddenly start shouting or speaking to no-one in particular. We also thought this was funny, until the therapist explained to us that because she was blind, she couldn't see who was talking or where sounds came from. She thought they were just around. So we had to teach her to first say our names before starting, like 'Ashley, I want you to help me…'

"We don't mind people staring anymore and sometimes I'll just say, "This is Chantelle. She's my sister and she's blind." Then people know and they stop wondering why she's different. After all, nobody is perfect.

"And that is all I have to say about Chantelle."

Activities for 6 to 8 year olds

How did Ashley and Chantelle feel?

Ask the children to think about Ashley and how she felt talking about her sister Chantelle. Ask the children to finish the sentence:

'I think Ashley felt...'

Now ask them to think about how Chantelle might feel if people were talking about her and her blindness.

Ask the children to finish the sentence,

'I think Chantelle would feel...'

Ask the children to think about how they would feel if they were blind. What kinds of things would they miss seeing? What would they miss most.

Ask the children to work in pairs, one with closed eyes and the other as the leader. Remind the 'leader' to make sure that they don't lead the 'blind' person into danger and ask them to move around the classroom, not bumping into anything. Change over.

Ashley might feel...

excited
important
good
sharing
enjoying telling
involved
pleased to talk.

Chantelle might feel...

nervous
hesitant
shy
uncertain
timid
anxious

Ask the children to come back into the circle and talk about how it felt to be led around and how it felt to have to lead someone around.

What is this?

Explain that today you want the children to experience being blind and eating food. Prepare a set of three or four foods under covers with disposable spoons. Ask the children to work in pairs with one feeding the other, who has their eyes tightly closed (or blindfolded). Ask them to remember what the tastes are. Change places.

In Circle Time ask volunteers to tell you what they thought the foods were – how many were right? Did anyone get any wrong?

Get Dressed

Ask the children to bring their outdoor clothes into the classroom. Working in pairs, ask one of each pair to 'dress' the other who is blindfolded or has eyes closed. In Circle Time ask volunteers to tell how it felt to need someone to help them to dress.

Ask them to finish the sentence:

'If I had a blind brother or sister, I would...'

Activities for 9 to 11 year olds

Explain to the children that you want them to experience some of the feelings of blind people. Ask the children first to experience writing without looking. Make sure they close their eyes and write a sentence. Is it legible? Can they read it?

How does it feel?

Prepare two sets of different textured fabrics in various colours in closed boxes. You might choose voile, corduroy, tweed, cotton, satin, wool.

Ask the children to work in pairs, one to be blindfolded and then to feel the first set of various fabrics. Ask the one who can see to write down what colour the person thinks each fabric is. Change places and use the other set of fabrics.

In Circle Time ask volunteers to explain their feelings about the fabrics – did any of them get the colours right? Can they get some idea of how a person who is blind might feel about colours?

Braille

Ask the children to think about never being able to read their favourite story and look at the illustrations. Ask volunteers to finish the sentence:

'If I couldn't read my favourite book I'd feel...'

Remind them that this is just how Chantelle would feel.

Ask the children if they know how blind people can read and ask any volunteer to talk about Braille.

Ask children to find out as much as they can about Braille, other aids for blind people, including guide dogs, famous blind people. Ask them to use books, encyclopedias, internet as well as talking to people at home. Make a display of their research findings to share with others in your school.

> In 1821 a French army captain, Charles Barbier, invented a system of point type, a code based on groups of dots.
>
> Louis Braille (1809-1852) was blind from the age of three and later became a French teacher of the blind. He adapted Barbier's system, using groups of one to six dots.

Samaya's Biggest Presents

6. Samaya's Biggest Presents

Information

This story is about Samaya, who has a hearing impairment. In it the children will learn how Samaya can be helped to hear with the help of hearing aids. The story also tells about the difficulties of born deaf children who have not learned to talk and their use of lip-reading and signing. Children will understand the need to face someone who is partially deaf and how empathetic friends can help someone who is deaf.

A hearing impairment can be conductive or sensorineural. The first is caused by a blockage in the ear, like wax or 'glue ear', which is usually temporary and can be treated medically.

Sensorineural hearing losses are generally caused by difficulties with the nerves which link to the ear and can affect one or both ears. This is usually permanent.

A child with conductive hearing loss may:

▸ have difficulty in listening, but give the impression
of being able to hear on occasions

▸ be a late talker with unclear speech

▸ seem insecure or confused in class

▸ say 'what?' or 'pardon' a lot as their hearing fluctuates

▸ speak loudly on occasions.

A child with sensorineural hearing loss may have difficulty:

▸ with certain sound frequencies

▸ complex structures of language.

A child with a hearing impairment will be helped if:

▸ she sits at the front of the class

▸ a classroom assistant ensures that she understands instructions

▸ people face her when talking to assist with lip-reading.

Useful books include:

Dare, A., O'Donovan, M. (1997) *Good Practice in Caring for Young Children with Special Needs*, Stanley Thornes, Cheltenham.

Stakes, Richard & Hornby, Garry. (1996) *Meeting Special Needs in Mainstream Schools*, David Fulton Publishers Ltd., London.

www.rnid.org.uk

The Website for the Royal National Institute for Deaf People. Information is provided about the Institute, services, projects and news. A range of information leaflets on topics such as common ear problems, benefits and services for deaf people, and how your ears work, are also available.

www.rnid.ord.uk/html/factsheets

www.hearingcenteronline.com/diction_def.shtml

www.rnid.org.uk/html/leaflets/basic_bsl.htm Introducing British Sign Language

This leaflet provides information about learning British Sign Language, grammar, fingerspelling, different languages in different countries, regional variations, and how to find out more. The leaflet is available as a text document or in PDF, which requires the Adobe Acrobat Reader. Published on the Web by the Royal National Institute for Deaf People (RNID).

LINKS

- ▶ hearing dogs for people who are deaf
- ▶ body language
- ▶ activities in the story of Marak.

Samaya's Biggest Presents

Not very long ago, a little girl named Samaya lived in a lovely house with her brothers and sisters. She was the youngest of the family and a very happy little girl who wanted to do everything that her brothers and sisters did. The only thing that was different about her was that she was quieter and calmer than the others.

One day, the children were playing hide-and-seek in the garden. When it was Samaya's turn to close her eyes, their mother saw that a rainstorm was brewing. She called them and said, "Children, come in! Look at the storm. You'll get wet."

Samaya's brothers and sisters ran into the house, but she still stood with her eyes closed. "Ten! I'm coming!" she shouted. She opened her lovely green eyes and started looking everywhere. She couldn't find anyone. She looked up into the sky and saw the angry black clouds.

Why did they run away from me? Why didn't they warn me? Where are they now? Lots of thoughts passed through Samaya's mind. Crying, Samaya ran into the house to find her mum.

"Why didn't you come in earlier, darling? Didn't you hear me calling you?" But Samaya just kept on crying.

Samaya's mum started watching her closely and realised that her little girl was not hearing well. When her brothers and sisters were at school, she sat quietly and played with Sammy, their big brown dog. But sometimes when Sammy whined to go outside, Samaya didn't hear him.

Samaya's mum decided to take Samaya to a speech therapist. She told the therapist all about the day of the storm and about Samaya not hearing Sammy when he whined. "Usually Samaya is such a good little girl, I wondered why she didn't listen to me?"

After carefully listening to the story the therapist said, "I think Samaya might be hearing impaired." The therapist put Samaya into a little booth, put headphones on her ears and said, "I want you to listen carefully. When you hear a mouse squeaking in your ear, I want you to put up your hand."

After seeing how she reacted to the different sounds, the therapist explained everything to Samaya's mum. "Samaya is not deaf," she said. "She has a hearing impairment. This means that sounds have to be very loud before she is able to hear them. I am going to put these hearing aids in her ears and that should help her. A hearing aid works exactly like a very fancy amplifier," the therapist continued. "It means that all the sounds around her are made much louder so that she can hear them. You will have to teach her how to use the hearing aids and how to listen."

Samaya's mum was very nervous. "How will I be able to do it all?"

"Don't be so worried, you will soon get used to the routine. Remember that Samaya is exactly the same as all your other children. She is not sick. She is not strange. She is not stupid. She only has a hearing impairment," the therapist said.

"Every time you hear a sound, you will have to draw her attention to the sound and tell her what it is. For example, when the pigeons wake you in the morning with their singing, make Samaya listen to the birdsong and tell her what it is. When an aeroplane passes, point to the sky and tell her what it is. You will also have to make sure that she watches your mouth when you speak to her, so that she can learn to read your lips. This will help her to know exactly what you are saying. It also means that you must never turn your back on Samaya when you speak to her or cover your mouth with your hand, as this will make it very difficult for her to understand you."

Samaya's mum was feeling more confident now and thanked the therapist for her help.

Soon, spending time with Samaya became a huge adventure. Her brothers and sister enjoyed teaching her what all the different sounds meant: a baby crying in a pram, a cricket, a ladybird, and especially the sounds that meant danger, like the dog's bark. Samaya felt that her hearing aids were the biggest present that she had ever received.

Then one day, while Samaya and her family visited the zoo, they saw something interesting. There, on a blanket sat a group of boys and girls who were almost the same age as Samaya, and a lady sat with them. But what fascinated Samaya was that the lady wasn't using her mouth to talk to them, she was making all kinds of interesting movements with her hands.

Samaya couldn't take her eyes off this lady and curiously she asked her mother, "What are they doing? Why is the lady making those signs? Doesn't she want to talk to them?"

Her mum laughed and explained, "They are deaf and they have to use their hands when they want to talk about something. Using your hands to communicate is called sign language."

Samaya was fascinated. "Why don't they go to the therapists and get hearing aids like me?" she asked.

"That is because they are deaf, not hearing impaired like you. It means that even if sounds are very loud, they will still be unable to hear them. Inside your ear you have three little hearing bones and a cochlea. That is something that looks like a snail's shell and it has a lot of tiny hair cells inside. When you hear a sound, it moves through your ear, through the three hearing bones and through the cochlea. The hair cells then take the sound to the hearing nerve, which makes you hear. If the hair cells fall flat, they can't carry the sound and you are deaf. Some deaf people might also get a cochlear implant. That means that the doctors give you a whole new electronic cochlea and then you are able to hear some sounds."

Samaya was still wondering about all of this. "So does that mean that nothing can make the hair cells stand upright again?"

"That's exactly right," her mum said. "Now in your case, the hair cells can still carry the sounds, if the sounds are made loud enough."

"Is that why the lady and the children use sign language?" Samaya asked.

"Mmm, some deaf people will learn to talk, but a lot of them need to use sign language to tell you what they want or how they feel. It doesn't matter what you use to communicate, the important thing is that you have some way of telling others what you want and think."

When the deaf children saw that Samaya was watching them and that she really wanted to understand what it was like to be deaf, they started signing to her. Samaya didn't understand what the signs meant, but the lady translated. "They want to know if you'll be their friend."

A huge smile crept over Samaya's face as she started nodding her head. "Yes of course I will! Will you teach me some of their signs?"

The children had a great afternoon in the park. Samaya turned to her mum and said, "My biggest present was my hearing aids, but my best present was making new friends. Even if they can't hear my voice, it is nice to have such friendly friends."

Activities for 6 to 8 year olds

Which bit of the story do you think is the most important?

In Circle Time, after you have read the story ask the children to close their eyes for a moment to think about this story. Ask them to go through the story stage by stage and re-tell it to you. Ask a volunteer to start and ask others to continue.

Then ask the children to think of the real issues in the story. Go around the circle asking them to finish the sentence:

'I think the most important part was…

Make a note of what the children say; when all have had a turn read through what they said. Ask the children to draw and write about the one they think is the most important and to give their reasons.

> **The important part was when:**
>
> she couldn't hear the storm
>
> Mum saw she couldn't hear
>
> she went to the speech therapist
>
> she was given the hearing aid
>
> her mum made her listen to birds
>
> she found out about signing
>
> she made new friends

Signs

In Circle Time talk to the children about signing and explain that there are specific signs that people who have a hearing impairment use when they want to talk. There are various sign languages; these four are natural signs. Help the children to learn these four.

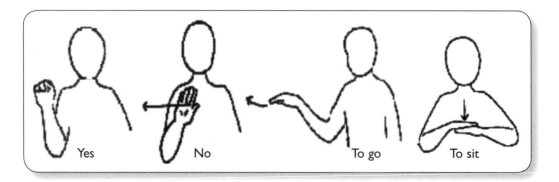

Ask the children to work in pairs and devise other signs that would be useful to someone who has a hearing impairment. Ask them to draw the signs and to write what they mean.

Ask the children to think about how friends could help a new girl, Samaya, to feel good about herself even though she found it difficult to hear. Ask them to think about the kinds of things good friends could do and say when she came to school for the first time with her hearing aids.

Activities for 9 to 11 year olds

Can you hear me?

In Circle Time talk about how we use the sound of words to understand what people are saying. Ask the children to speak without any sound at all. Ask them to say their name.

Ask the children to finish this sentence – without any sound at all.

'My name is…'

When everyone has had a turn, talk about the difficulty of hearing what people say when there is no sound. Did they all look very carefully at the person speaking? How many of them could make out the words?

Now go around the circle and ask each child to say their own short silent sentence. Ask volunteers to say what they thought the child said.

Ask the children to work in pairs and try to hold a conversation without words.

> **Samaya would have to:**
>
> watch the person's mouth
>
> be face to face with them
>
> think hard about what they mean
>
> ask them to talk slowly
>
> ask them to talk clearly
>
> watch their body language
>
> watch their gestures

Come back to the circle and talk about the difficulties they had. Did some of the children use gestures to help their talk? Talk about how this can help people to understand.

Ask the children to write a few sentences about the difficulties that Samaya would have in trying to communicate.

Body Language

Ask the children to find a space in the classroom so that they have plenty of room to move their limbs. Tell them that they are going to communicate without words and ask them to keep their mouths firmly closed and, using their body and limbs communicate:

- no
- yes
- thank you
- I'm angry
- I'm very happy
- go away
- come here.

In the circle talk about the need to use gesture in ballet and in mime and ask the children to work in pairs to devise a simple 'conversation' between themselves. Explain that they must try to remember what they 'say' and do as you will want some to show their mime. Ask the children to practise and then ask volunteers to show their mime. Can the other children guess what they are 'saying?'

The Active Boy

7. The Active Boy

Information

This story is about Jordan who has Attention Deficit Hyperactivity Disorder (ADHD). Such children can be thought of as difficult and a nuisance and this story emphasises that this condition has a cause which needs careful and sympathetic treatment in the classroom. The story shows the children that they have a role to play in understanding ADHD and accepting Jordan as he is.

ADHD is a disorder with an underlying biological cause. It is a treatable (not curable) complex disorder which affects approximately 3 to 6 percent of the population.

ADHD:

- is a treatable disorder which when appropriately handled can be well controlled
- always has the same components: impulsiveness, inattention and hyperactivity
- is a disorder that seems to exist in varying degrees of severity in different people
- has no definitive diagnostic test and the symptoms vary according to the age of the child, circumstances and varying situations
- children have a brain that functions in a characteristic way and as a result behave and experience life in a different way from non-ADHD children.

Children may present as:

- having difficulty following instructions
- having difficulty sustaining attention and appearing not to listen
- failing to give close attention to detail
- often being disorganised and losing things
- making careless mistakes
- being unmotivated to complete school work.

Useful books include:

Munden, Alison and Arcelus (1999), *Jon, The AD/HD Handbook*, Jessica Kingsley Publishers, London.

Cooper, P. and Ideus, K. (1996) *Attention Deficit/Hyperactivity Disorder, A Practical Guide for Teachers*, David Fulton Publishers Ltd, London.

Gordon, M. & Parker, H. *Teaching the Child with ADHD: A Slide Program for In-Service Training.*

Holowenko, H. (1999) *Attention Deficit/Hyperactivity Disorder: A Multidisciplinary Approach*, Jessica Kingsley, Publishers, London.

There are many useful websites including;

www.addfocus.co.uk

www.therapy-in-praxis.ltd.co.uk

The Active Boy

He woke right in the middle of a dream; it was usually much better to finish the dream and then wake up – that way you knew the ending. This dream didn't have an ending. It just went on and on and on. In the dream Jordan was about two years younger than he was now and he had only been in school for a year.

He was looking up at the three most important people in his life, Dad, Auntie Grace and his teacher, Miss Edie. They were all towering above him, looking down with weary, impatient and disappointed faces and they were saying, "Keep still!", "Stop fidgeting!", "Concentrate on what you are doing!"

It was just like a stuck record and Jordan didn't think it would ever end. He had lots of good intentions and then, before he knew it, somebody was saying something like, "I despair of you!" or "How many times do I have to tell you?" They might as well ask him to see in the pitch dark or fly to Disneyworld or stop the earth turning at midday so it was always light.

The funny thing was that he couldn't remember when it turned from good to bad, when his Dad stopped saying so proudly that he was a very active baby and started saying he was over-active and then HYPERACTIVE! It had something to do with seeing that doctor. They spent hours at the clinic in town. Different people talked to Dad and Auntie Grace whilst he did lots of games and words and maths. Luckily they kept changing the activity to different things so he could bear it. He finished first and whilst he waited for Dad he ran up and down the passage and went into the toilets to turn on all the taps. He was just about to run around the car park and flip all the wing mirrors, a favourite activity because it saved them from breaking if a car crashed into them, when the doctor's door opened and she invited Jordan to join them.

She was kind and she explained that Jordan was not naughty – he couldn't help himself without a lot of support and a lot of new learning. She told him that his behaviour was called Attention Deficit Hyperactivity Disorder – ADHD for short. This meant that he didn't focus on just one thing at a time. He would watch and listen and notice everything at the same time. She told him that his behaviour used to be very useful in the olden days.

"Do you mean before they invented colour?" asked Jordan.

The doctor looked very puzzled and frowned. "What do you mean, Jordan?"

"Well, in all the old films everything is black and white and then they invented colour and the new films are much better."

The doctor laughed and she explained that the world was always in colour, but film techniques weren't advanced enough to make colour pictures.

"Anyway, Jordan, we are talking about even further back before we had films and cameras. We are talking about the time when humans were hunters, when they had to chase and kill their food and when the earth was a very hard and dangerous place to be. In those days people like you, Jordan, were the best hunters, the first to spot danger. Because they were so active and alert they were the most likely to survive."

"Then things changed and humans learned how to make machinery, to grow crops and farm the land and the animals for food. Then people like you, Jordan, were less likely to be successful. What was needed in the new era was patience, concentration and perseverance. It took such a long time to make some wheat seeds become a loaf of bread."

Jordan sighed. How would he fit in when he could never wait for his Auntie Grace to cook his toast, let alone grow it? He must have looked really sad because Dad gave him a friendly nudge on the shoulder and Auntie Grace said, "Don't worry too much, love. We will help you – there are lots of things we can try."

"We will write to your teachers and all together we will make a plan for you. You are not a naughty boy – you are an active boy in a world that isn't very active. We will start by helping you to learn to concentrate just for a short while and we promise not to tell you off if it is not always possible. We know you will do your best. With your permission we can explain some of this to the other children in the class so that they can help you."

Jordan nodded. It was worth a try, he thought.

By the next term Jordan had settled into his new class with his new teacher, Mr Maddock. The teacher knew all about ADHD people because he had a nephew who had it too. Jordan was allowed to use a timer and set his concentration blocks for six minutes, then he could move about quietly for a minute before starting work again. He was allowed to work on a table by himself if he preferred and he had a red flag on his desk. If he waved it someone from his circle of friends would come and sit with him and help him.

On one hot Friday afternoon Mr Maddock settled the class for storytime – it was the last chapter of Harry Potter and the Chamber of Secrets and everyone was very excited to hear the ending… except Jordan. He knew the ending – Auntie Grace had already read it to him. He liked to listen to stories whilst he did Lego or sat in the bath playing with the water. He never, never, never liked to sit still!

The windows were wide open and Jordan paced quietly up and down the edge of the room, half listening and half pretending that he was outside running round the field. Suddenly he saw a grey cloud in the distance, coming towards the school. No – it wasn't a cloud – what was it?

As it got nearer Jordan could hear that it was buzzing. It was bees, a big swarm. Jordan had read about them in the papers.

"Shut the windows everyone – quick, quick!" he shouted. Mr Maddock calmly asked him to be quiet and went on reading.

"Sir, sir, it is important – look at the bees." He said, waving his red flag in the air.

"Shut the windows everybody, as fast as you can, please!" said Mr Maddock, not quite as calm as usual.

Only three bees got into the room and the rest settled on the glass like a black curtain. Everyone relaxed and nobody was stung. A local beekeeper in a netting hood came to take the bees away to a hive.

Auntie Grace embroidered a big bee on Jordan's flag so that nobody would forget how useful it was in the hands of an active boy.

Activities for 6 to 8 year olds

Statues

Remind the children of the story of Jordan and explain that his brain is wired differently from most people's. Talk about the difficulty that Jordan had – he really couldn't make himself keep still for very long.

Ask the children to find a partner and start by being very active - stand up, jump up and down three times and then sit down and keep really still. Tell them they mustn't move a muscle. Ask them to note how long they can keep still. Use the classroom clock or a stopwatch to see when the first person moves.

In Circle Time talk about how difficult it is to keep really still. Is there a difference between boys and girls?

Ask the children to finish this sentence:

'When I try to keep still, I...'

Two things at the same time

In Circle Time ask the children to see if they can rub their tummy and pat their head at the same time. Ask the children to think of other things that they can do at the same time. Ask volunteers to give their suggestions for you to write up.

Talk about how useful it is for people to be able to do several things at the same time. Tell them that this is called multi-tasking. Ask the children to think of a Saturday at home and the multi-tasking that their parents do. Ask them to write down a description of a parent or carer doing several things at the same time, for example, cooking a meal, laying the table, talking to a baby, listening to TV, watching the vegetables don't boil over.

> **Two things at once**
>
> I can draw and listen to TV.
>
> I can talk and do PE.
>
> I can listen to music and write.
>
> I can draw when I'm on the phone.
>
> My mum can knit and read.
>
> My dad can clean the car and listen to the radio.

Explain that multi-tasking is what the active boy was doing – being aware of many things and concentrating on more than one thing at the same time. Remind the children that Jordan had a specific condition and could not help moving about. Explain that he needs to have his day's work planned so that he could do his best in a different way from them. Remind them that being cross with a person with ADHD doesn't help and that children such as Jordan need our understanding and help.

Activities for 9 to 11 year olds

Timers

In Circle Time remind the children about Jordan. Talk about how his brain worked differently from other people and that he needed to have his work planned so that he could work in short bursts.

Explain that this morning you are going to time them at work. Ask the children to say how long they think they will need to complete the task. Then say you will allow them exactly half that time. Make sure the children finish exactly on your time.

Come together in a circle and ask volunteers to say how they felt when they had to stop. Make a note of their responses on a flip-chart or chalkboard. Talk about these feelings. Now ask the children to think about Jordan who was just the opposite of them. He got easily bored and needed to change activities frequently.

Working to time

I couldn't get started.

I lost my ideas.

I didn't have time to get the materials.

Too little time is a waste of time.

I felt angry I couldn't finish.

I felt sad about my unfinished work.

Ask the children if they can think of ways to help an active child in your class. What would they say when the child needed to change activities?

Multi-tasking

In Circle Time ask the children to think about people who have to do several things at the same time. Do people always stop what they are doing when something else has to be done? Ask volunteers to tell you some of the jobs that need multi-tasking and prioritising, such as watching to see a baby is safe while watching TV, listening to the radio while driving a car – which has priority?

Ask them to finish the sentence, 'At the same time I can do...and...'

Ask them to write about multi-tasking that they do, saying which is the priority.

Choose a quiet and calm piece of music to play and ask the children to try multi-tasking by listening to the music at the same time as doing their next piece of work and keeping one eye on the clock. Come together in Circle Time and talk about how it feels to do several things at the same time.

Remind them about Jordan and how he had the ability to think about and do several things at the same time. Explain that there will be times when we all need to do this, but that sometimes we need to concentrate on one important task. Jordan is learning to do this, but it is something he finds hard to control and that we must understand his difficulties.

Akuti's Magic Talking Machine

8. Akuti's Magic Talking Machine

Information

This is a story about Akuti who was badly hurt in a road accident. She spent a long time in hospital and because she was unable to talk, she was eventually given a talking machine. The children will have many questions about Akuti in hospital and the various treatments.

The story lends itself to work about accidents, hospitals, road safety and the suggested activities support this. You may be able to investigate your local hospital A&E facilities and find out about intensive care, support systems, physiotherapy, occupational therapy and speech therapy.

You could invite health professionals to school to extend this work and include your road safety officer, school nurse/doctor as well as any parents or carers who work in this field.

Books for younger children include:

Titles from the 'My school' series published by Wayland Publishers, Hove, UK. These include The Lollipop Man and The Road Safety Officer.

Websites include:

www.rospa.com where you will find teaching materials on road safety.

LINKS with:

- people in the news who have had accidents or illness which have left them unable to speak, for example, 'Superman' Christopher Reeve

- people who are deaf and dumb

- other new technology that enables disabled people to live a more normal life

- road safety.

8. Akuti's Magic Talking Machine

Hi! My name is Akuti. I live in a house with my mum, dad and younger sister Sunita. I was involved in a car accident about 5 years ago when I was only two years old. I can't remember anything about the accident, but my dad says that the other car didn't stop at a red traffic light and that it was a huge collision. Fortunately the ambulance arrived very quickly and I was taken to hospital. Hospital became my 'new home' and I spent almost 6 months there!

At first I was in a coma, which lasted for 10 days. My mum and dad were very worried as I was lying very still with my eyes closed and didn't seem to react when they spoke to me or even to the sound of the siren of my favorite fire engine. Then I gradually became more and more aware of everything going on around me. Eventually after the medical problems had been cleared up, like the difficulties I had with breathing due to a broken rib that punctured my lung, my right leg that was broken in three different places and all the bruising, the doctor said I must go for 'rehab' – this is short for rehabilitation. This means that a speech therapist, an occupational therapist and a physiotherapist all came to see me and gave me all kinds of activities and exercises to do. Actually, they didn't really give them to me to do them on my own, but they showed Mum and Dad what they had to do to get my body working again.

Since the crash, my brain doesn't work in the same way it did before. When you hit your head very hard, like in an accident, your brain moves around banging on all the different parts of your skull, causing problems in the different parts of the brain. That means that not only one part of the brain, like the speaking, moving or seeing part is affected, but rather that more than one part may be damaged. If you had to look at an X-Ray of my brain, you would see lots of little specks all over it. That is where the damage happened.

This means that when I try to use my legs, my brain doesn't send the message to the muscles to move, so I need a wheelchair to get around. My right leg works a bit better than the left leg, but not enough for me to walk. Some of my friends at school use crutches or braces that help them to walk. In some ways I am very lucky. The part of my brain that helps me think and learn new things is fine! So I can think just like you, and I know what and whom I like or don't like.

Some days I get really angry and sad when the people around me do not understand what I am trying to say to them. I try hard to say the words, but my lips and tongue can't make the movements that I want them to make. You see, the message from my brain to 'talk loud and clear' does not get to the muscles in my mouth, so the words come out strangely. But I can understand everything you say! Mum told me that there are lots of different reasons why children might not be able to talk, for example, they might have autism or cerebral palsy, or they might have Down's syndrome.

People sometimes stare at me when my mum pushes me in my wheelchair at the shops. I can see that they think that I am dumb because I can't speak. A few of them even ask Mum silly questions about me as if I don't understand what they are saying! Most people think that because I can't speak clearly, they can't speak to me. This can make me feel very lonely!

I like it when Sunita's friends come to play. They are very nice to me, but I wish that I could also have my own friends to play. I could show them my computer! But it is hard to make friends when people don't understand you when you speak.

Every morning my mum picks me up from my bed and helps me into my wheelchair. She helps me to get dressed and to have breakfast. My arms have jerky movements that I can't control and this makes it hard to do things like hold a spoon or a pen. I can make complicated things, like build a helicopter with my Lego, but someone has to help me and it takes a very long time. Sometimes I do hold a spoon or cup by myself, but not when we're in a hurry to get ready for school! The mini-bus from my school fetches me right outside my house and takes me to school.

The other day, instead of going to school, Mum said that we were going to see some people at the university clinic who would show me some other ways to 'talk'. I did not believe that there were other ways of talking except by saying things with your mouth! But I was very excited because I thought that maybe they could show me how to talk to other children so that I could make some new friends.

I was really nervous, but they were very helpful and friendly at the clinic where my mum took me. One of thewomen asked my mum a whole lot of questions about the family and me. I went into another room with a lady called Jane. We had fun playing with lots of different toys and paging through books. Then she showed me one of the most wonderful things I have ever seen! A talking machine!

On the top part of the machine were a lot of pictures of different things. Jane showed me how to press a button using 'Peter Pointer' on my right hand because that is the hand, which works the best. When I pressed the button with the 'ball' picture on, a voice said: "Please play ball with me." I could not believe my ears! I pressed the button of a boy shaking his head and it said, "No, I don't want that one."

I really wanted to take the machine home, so I pressed the button with the picture of 'please' and the voice said, "Please may I?" "May you what? asked Jane. I pointed to the machine. Jane immediately understood what I wanted and said we could take the machine home for the weekend. She smiled and said if we liked it and it helped me she would order one for me. I could see that my mum was also very excited when she heard that!

I practised hard all afternoon I could use all the pictures to make the machine talk and I could put two pictures together. I tried it on my Mum. First I pressed "I want..." and then I pressed "drink". She laughed and got me some juice.

When dad got home from work I played a trick on him! As he came through the door I pressed the button with the picture of 'hi!' He turned and looked behind him to see who was saying hello to him! So I pressed 'hi!' again. This time he asked mum who had said, "hi!" Mum, Michelle and I started laughing and Mum explained that it was my amazing talking machine! Dad was so pleased that I had to show him all the buttons!

Soon I will have my very own talking machine that can go everywhere with me. One day you may see me at the shops. You may even see someone like me in your school someday. Come over and chat to me! It hurts more to be ignored or stared at than to be asked questions about myself. If you talk to me, it shows me that you care!

Activities for 6 to 8 year olds

Akuti's feelings

In Circle Time, ask the children to think about this story and about and how Akuti must have felt when her mum takes her out in her special chair and people stare at her.

Ask the children to finish the sentence:

'I think Akuti would feel…'

Collect the words and phrases the children give and make a chart of them.

Ask the children to think about what they could do to make Akuti feel better about having this brain condition. Ask volunteers to finish the sentence:

'I could…'

> **Akuti could feel:**
>
> angry
>
> different
>
> sad
>
> awkward
>
> the same inside
>
> not a baby
>
> frustrated
>
> annoyed
>
> upset
>
> She wants to say 'I can hear. I'm not stupid.'

Road Safety

The story doesn't tell how the accident happened.

Ask the children to think about road safety and accidents and to finish this sentence:

'Accidents on the road happen when…'

Ask the children to think of their part in keeping safe when they are walking along the pavement, about safe places to cross roads, about safety when playing on such things as bikes, skates or skateboards.

Ask children to finish the sentence:

'I can keep safe near roads when I…'

Ask the children to close their eyes and think of their part in keeping safe when they are in a car. And ask volunteers to say what they do to keep safe.

Activities for 9 to 11 year olds

I can talk!

Ask the children to think about Akuti's feelings when she got her new machine and could talk to people.

Ask them to finish the sentence:

'I think Akuti would feel...'

As them to mime her body language and facial expression.

Ask the children to think what Akuti would say to her family when she first got her talking machine. Ask them to finish the sentence:

'I think Akuti would say...'

> **Akuti would feel:**
>
> excited
>
> joyful
>
> ecstatic
>
> over the moon
>
> overjoyed
>
> elated
>
> **She'd say:**
>
> 'I can talk!'
>
> 'I'm like everyone else.'
>
> 'I'm not different.'
>
> 'I can ask for things.'

Accidents don't happen

In Circle Time talk to the children about accidents and how they are caused by something not going to plan. Explain that accidents are usually the result of someone not taking care or not thinking about 'what could happen if...'

Talk to the children about risk – about assessing risks and about whether you can minimise them and go ahead or whether you should not do the thing that is risky.

Ask the children to draw someone doing something risky. Ask them to write down the risk, what the person could do to minimise the risk and whether the person should stop or whether they can make the situation safe enough to go ahead.

When all the children have finished their drawing and writing ask them to come to the circle and tell the rest of the class what they have drawn. You may like to make a display of these risky situations. Are they all real risks or are some fantasy risks?

Road Safety

In Circle Time ask the children to finish one of these three sentences:

'When I'm out on my own near roads, I can...to keep safe.'

'The safe places to play are...'

'The danger spots near roads are...'

Remind the children about the importance fo keeping safe. Explain that an accident can happen in a moment but the effects can last all your life.

Not at Home

9. Not at Home

Information

This story is about Martha who is not living in her own home. For some reason she is living elsewhere and is going to a different school. There are many reasons why children have to leave home and live elsewhere – sometimes there is a family crisis, parents are not available to look after their children. The reasons are not part of this story, which is concerned with the feelings of a child who is suddenly thrust into a different environment.

Local authorities are responsible for care of children whose needs cannot be met at home or when they might be at risk of significant harm. Some children may be in care with the agreement of their parents but when the local authority has not been able to work with parents the authority will go to court to remove children. Some can be looked after by their extended family such as aunts, uncles and grandparents. When this is not possible local authorities use foster carers.

Foster carers are carefully vetted and placed on registers and there will be a social worker to liaise between all parties. Some foster places are available for emergency fostering.

When children arrive in foster care they may be frightened and confused. They may have left their home suddenly with few clothes or toys. They may have difficulty in forming a relationship with their carers, may wet the bed and be anxious about this. Foster children will have had various backgrounds and may need a considerable time to settle in to their new home before they can relate to their carers. Schools which accept children who are suddenly fostered need to be aware of the special needs of such children.

Many websites exist which cater for various geographical areas of the UK.

www.fostering.com

www.barnardos.org.uk offers teachers' resources.

www.baaf.org.uk/pages/publish/books_fostachild.htm for useful books

Email addresses include:

foster.winchester@cathchild.org

foster.littlehampton@cathchild.org

foster.dartford@cathchild.org

LINK with:

- ▶ evacuees in the second world war
- ▶ bereavement
- ▶ orphans in the UK, from AIDS victims or from third world countries
- ▶ Dr Barnado's
- ▶ the story of Marak and activities

Note: If you know that you have a looked after child in your your class, it is important that you talk to him or her privately about this activity beforehand.

Not at Home

All the time she was at school she tried to pretend everything was normal. She didn't talk to any of her friends about what had happened because it felt as though that would make it 'real' and she wasn't ready to do that yet. Mrs Parry, the head, knew all about it but she never mentioned anything and that made Martha feel even less confident…as though it was something never to be talked about!

Jenny who came in to school to cook the dinners knew because she lived two doors away from Martha…NO! – she lived two doors away from where Martha used to live. She was kind but she put on a sad face when they met and called her 'poor kid'.

The worst times were when they did things in school about news and had to say what they had done at the weekend or where they were going during the holidays. Martha used to say nothing but she got into trouble.

"Come on Martha, surely you can think of something to say about the long summer holiday – it was six weeks after all! Have you forgotten everything?" complained Mr Herbert, her teacher.

Of course she could have said some stuff about the coach trip to the Seaton for the day or the cycle ride and the picnic…but it wasn't the same as the things she used to do as a family when they all went to stay with Gran and Grandad and her cousin was there too.

The best thing was to make up some lies and call it 'using her imagination'. So after a few weeks Martha just used her wishes to make her news.

For a while it worked. Life was a bit sad and a bit dull. She never accepted invitations to parties or out to stay overnight with a friend because she couldn't invite anybody back. She held back from making really good friends with anybody, kids or grown-ups, because they would probably go away sometime. Gradually Martha withdrew into what felt like a cloudy space where the most colourful and fun times were the daydreaming and reality was just grey. She realised that you didn't have to be alone to feel lonely – in fact you could be very lonely surrounded by people if they weren't the right people.

She coped until one dreadful, dreadful day when everyone was asked to make a collage pattern out of beads and glitter and seeds. It was to be stuck onto a folded piece of stiff paper to make a mother's day card.

Martha sat and sat and did nothing. She felt nothing. She was not going to make this card. For the first time in school she felt the tears stinging her eyes – not quiet ears, big howling, trembling, choking tears and once they started they didn't stop, not for ages. Eventually Mr Herbert sent the rest of the children out to play early and he sat close to Martha – she leaned against him because all that howling had exhausted her. He didn't ask her for any details and she didn't explain – he just said that he could see she was very unhappy and that he would arrange for her to have some talk-time with Helen, the school nurse, who often spent time with children, even when they weren't sick.

It took many weeks for Martha to come out of the grey clouds. It was one day when Helen said to her, "It is OK to feel sad about not living with your family. You will probably feel sad even when you are an old woman. People can survive sadness. But it is not OK to think that you can change it by wishing or dreaming. That is not your responsibility and it is not within your power."

Two weeks later Helen did something called a Circle of Friends for Martha. With her agreement she told the rest of the class about how Martha's life had changed and asked for some kids to think of ways they could help Martha. They came up with lots of ideas and soon she was invited to parties and included without anyone expecting that she could invite them back. One friend asked her to join her family on a camping holiday in the New Forest.

Martha is now an old woman with grown-up children and three grandchildren so she has a family of her own. She is still sad that her parents were not in her life but she is used to it and it doesn't make her life grey any more.

Activities for 6 to 8 year olds

Away from home

In Circle Time talk with the children about times they have spent away from home. Ask the children to think about sleepovers. Ask them to finish one of these two sentences:

'I went to a sleepover and I felt...'

'I haven't been to a sleepover because...'

Talk about going to stay in someone's house for a few nights, without their parents or family. Ask the children to wave a hand if they have stayed overnight in someone else's house. Ask them to stand in various places if they:

> ▸ have never stayed in someone's house

> ▸ have stayed overnight in someone's house with their own parents there

> ▸ have stayed overnight in someone else's house without their own parents.

Count up the numbers and note these down.

Ask volunteers to tell you how they felt when they slept in someone else's house without their parents.

> **Away from home**
>
> 22 of us have been on sleepovers.
>
> 12 of us have never stayed away without our parents.
>
> 10 of us stayed in a family house without our family.
>
> 5 of us stayed in someone else's house without our parents or family.

Martha's feelings

Talk to the children about how Martha would be feeling when she had to go and live somewhere else without her family.

Ask the children to finish the sentence:

'I think Martha would be feeling...'

Ask the children to think about how Martha would be feeling on her first day at a different school and to finish the sentence:

'I think Martha would be feeling...'

Ask the children to think about what they could do to help Martha to feel better about being in a different school.

Ask volunteers to say what they could do to help. Make a list of all the things the children say and ask them to draw a picture of them doing one of those things.

Activities for 9 to 11 year olds

The worst things

Ask the children to think back to the story of Martha and to tell you the main points of the story.

Jot down keywords on the chalkboard or flip-chart.

Ask the children to think what would be the worst thing for Martha about not being in her old home and to finish the sentence:

'I think the worst thing would be...'

How would I feel? What could I do?

Ask the children to think about how they would feel if they were suddenly plucked from their family and home and had to go to live in a strange place with someone else.

Ask them what they would miss the most and to finish the sentence:

'I would miss...'

> **The worst things for Martha...**
>
> telling what she did at weekends
>
> talking about holidays
>
> people saying 'poor kid'
>
> not going to people's parties
>
> feeling lonely
>
> Mothers Day
>
> feeling really sad and empty
>
> missing her own family
>
> missing her school
>
> missing her friends

Collect the children's responses, making a brief list on the board. Ask the children to read through the list and try to decide what would be the very worst thing about such a situation. Give each child one vote and write the scores against their list.

Talk again about Martha's story and how she felt excluded in her new school. Do they recognise that the children in Martha's school could have helped her?

Ask them to think about what they could do if they had a situation like this in your classroom. Ask them to write about what they could do and to illustrate their work. You could share this work with other classes by writing up the main points of the story in large print and displaying the children's work around it.

Marak

10. Marak

Information

This story is about Marak, a refugee from another country who is unable to speak English when he first goes to an English speaking school. In these days of asylum seekers and refugees coming to the UK it is essential that children understand how the children of these people feel and understand that children who are asylum seekers or refugees have the same rights and entitlements as other children.

The government has allocated places for asylum seekers to go to. Some are special areas where schooling is provided. In time, accepted people will permeate local communities and need our help. Children have a vital role to play in helping others such as Marak integrate into the community.

Situations such as this highlight the necessity for all schools to have procedures in place to help foreign children to integrate. Special language teaching will need to be provided, with someone to interpret on initial entry to school. Children will need help to integrate and feel accepted in their UK school.

NCH, the children's charity states on their website:

"Asylum seeking and refugee children should receive an education within mainstream schools and not separately within accommodation centres if they live in them, though it may be appropriate to offer them and their families additional educational support in the centres, for example, English language teaching for those who do not speak English."

Alison Davies, director of Save the Children Scotland, said:

"Starting again in Glasgow has been a tremendous challenge for these children, which they have met with great courage. They speak of how they have been helped by the warmth and generosity of their new teachers and classmates as well as the Scottish people who have welcomed them here."

Useful books include:

Allen, P., Warwick, I., Begum, J. (2004) *You are Welcome*, Lucky Duck Publishing, Bristol.

There are several useful websites:

www.nchafe.org.uk

LINKS with: 'Not at Home' story and activities

'Akuti's Talking Machine' activities

Citizenship and democracy.

Marak

His mum gently pushed him into the classroom and walked away – everyone knew that there was a new boy starting school today and they knew that he didn't speak very good English.

'Why not?' they asked Ms Karakis.

"Well, he and his family have just arrived in this country. His name is Marak and he is nine years old. He hasn't had the chance to learn English yet. That is about all I know. We should make him feel very welcome and maybe we will get to know him better soon."

Marak stood in the doorway with his head down. He didn't move and he didn't raise his head when Ms Karakis spoke to him. She gently put her hand on her shoulder and guided him to a place on the carpet. He sat quite still and silently during the story and didn't look at anyone. Just before breaktime Ms Karakis put some music on. This was the signal for everyone to line up and walk along the corridor to the playground. Marak didn't stay in line – he jostled his way outside and walked towards the gate where he stood looking up and down the road as though he was waiting for someone. A few kids stared but mostly they ignored him. At the end of break a teacher had to go and encourage Marak back into the classroom. The same thing happened every day. Marak stood by the gate patiently waiting but nobody knew what he was waiting for.

When Marak had been in school for about a week a visitor arrived and he spent some time talking to Marak in a different language. Marak chatted to him – this was the first time the children in his class had heard his voice. The visitor asked Marak something and he nodded. Then they both walked to the front of the class and Ms Karakis invited them to talk.

"I am Thanasis and this is Marak. We come from the same country and we speak the same language. The difference is that I have been here for many years and I also speak English and German so I can help Marak communicate whilst he has some time to learn a new language. Now Marak wants to say 'hello' to you."

Marak stepped forward shyly and said a few words that nobody understood…Thanasis translated for him. Marak said. "Hello everybody, I am pleased to be here." After just a moment of silence Ms Karakis smiled at Marak and said, "Hello Marak – we are pleased to welcome you to our school!" and then all the children called out, 'Hello, Marak, Hi Marak!"

Marak smiled and his whole face changed, his eyes smiled and he looked around the class at all the friendly faces. Thanasis stepped forward.

"Marak and his family are refugees and that means that they had to leave our home country because it was not safe for them to go on living there. Marak's mother has been working to change the law that allows the government to put children into adult prisons and now she is in trouble so they all left in a hurry and came here. They have applied for permission to stay here but they have to wait to find out if it will be allowed. Whilst they are waiting Marak will come to school here and he will learn to speak English if we all help him. The best thing to do is always talk to Marak and whilst you are talking try to show him in other ways what the words mean. For example, if you offer him a sweet, hold the sweet out for him to see, if you want to take him to dinner then point to the dining hall. You will think of lots of ways to show him what you mean. By the way, Marak is very good at basketball and chess. I have to go now but I will come and visit again in two weeks. Bye."

Almost everything changed for Marak because everyone changed the way they behaved towards him. They wanted him to join in. They even started a chess club. It was going to be a long time before Marak and his family would know about their future and it was a difficult time. Sometimes Marak would drift towards the gate and look solemnly up and down the road, but mostly he was in amongst the other children, playing and talking in a mixture of English and his own language. Gradually his speech became more and more English, but not completely. He decided not to speak completely English until he was sure he could stay in England for a long time.

Activities for 6 to 8 year olds

How would you feel?

After reading the story in Circle Time, ask the children to think about how they would feel if they had to go to school where everyone spoke a different language. Ask the children to finish the sentence:

'I think I would feel…'

Make a note of their responses.

Talk with the children about these feelings and about what they could do to help Marak feel wanted and accepted by them all. Explain that it is not enough just to understand Marak's problem with communication, they have to actively help such a person to fit in and feel comfortable in their school and play.

I think I would feel…
strange
awful
horrible
left out
unwanted
upset inside
angry I couldn't understand
angry I couldn't talk
I couldn't join in
I wouldn't know what to do

A new country

Ask the children to think about how it would feel to have to leave home in a hurry and go to a new country to be safe.

Ask them what they would want to take with them. Ask them to finish the sentence:

'I would want to take…'

Ask the children to think about what they would miss most about this country, if they had to go and live somewhere else. Ask them to finish the sentence:

'I would miss…'

Ask the children to draw themselves in this country and to try to put in their picture all the things they most like about living here.

Activities for 9 to 11 year olds

Signs and body language

After reading this story to the children ask them to think about what they could do if a non-English speaking child came to your class. Ask them to think of ways to communicate with someone who doesn't understand the language. Talk about body language and the language of gestures.

Ask them to work in pairs and to devise some signs that could mean 'please', 'thank you', 'I'm happy', 'I want something'. Ask them to think of four other signs that someone like Marak could use.

Ask them to practise these signs and when they have got them right, to draw their signs with an explanation. After sharing their signs with others in their group ask them to leave their signs on their table with one person to explain them and to go around the classroom and look at other people's signs.

Come together in Circle Time and talk about which of the new signs would be useful to someone who couldn't understand English.

Human rights

Talk with the children about people who live in countries where people are not free to live as they please. Talk about displaced persons and how they may have to leave their homes in order to stay alive. Talk about any of these issues that are in the news today.

Talk about human rights and how lucky we are to live in a democratic country where we have these rights.

Ask the children to tell you what rights people should have in any country. Ask them to finish the sentence:

'I think we all have a right to…'

Make a list of all the things they say and ask if the children can put them into some kind of order. You could display this list together with pictures under a title of the children's choice, for example, 'Children's rights'.

Children's Rights
We have a right to…
be safe
clean water
food
clothes
somewhere to live
someone to love us
go to school
somewhere to play
health care and hospitals

Useful contacts and addresses in South Africa

Centre for Augmentative and Alternative Communication (CAAC)

Postal address:
CAAC
University of Pretoria
0002 Pretoria
Tel: (012) 420-2001
Fax: (012) 420-4389
E-Mail: juan.Bornman@up.ac.za
Web: www.up.ac.za/academic/caac

Office on the Status of Disabled People (OSDP0

Postal address:
The Presidency
Private bag X100
0001 Pretoria
Tel: (012) 300-5480
Fax: 9012) 300 – 5774
E-Mail: sebenzile@po.gov.za

Autism South Africa

Postal address:
PO Box 84209
2034 Greenside
Tel: (011) 486-3696
Fax: (011) 486-2619
E-Mail: autismsa@iafrica.com

South African National Council for the Blind

Postal address:
PO Box 11149
0028 Hatfield
Tel: (012) 346-1171
Fax: (012) 346-1149
E-Mail: admin@sancb.org.za

Deaf Federation of South Africa

Postal address:
Private Bag
2142 Westhoven
Tel: (011) 482-1610
Fax: (011) 726-5873
E-Mail: deafsa@icon.co.za

Down Syndrome South Africa

Postal address:
PO Box 12962
0028 Hatfield
Tel: (012) 345-4581
Fax: (012) 345-4581
E-Mail: dssaoffice@icon.co.za

National Association for persons with Cerebral Palsy

Postal address:
PO Box 426
2109 Melville
Tel: (011) 726-8040
Fax: (011) 726-5705
E-Mail: autismsa@iafrica.com

Disabled Children's Action Group (DICAG)

Postal address:
16 Broad road
7800 Wynberg
Tel: (021) 797-5977
Fax: (021) 797-5077
E-Mail: dicag@iafrica.com

Don't forget to visit our website for all our latest publications, news and reviews.

www.luckyduck.co.uk

New publications every year on our specialist topics:

- ▸ **Emotional Literacy**
- ▸ **Self-esteem**
- ▸ **Bullying**
- ▸ **Positive Behaviour Management**
- ▸ **Circle Time**
- ▸ **Anger Management**
- ▸ **Asperger's Syndrome**
- ▸ **Eating Disorders**